BASS HANON

75 EXERCISES TO BUILD ENDURANCE & FLEXIBILITY FOR BASS GUITAR PLAYERS

BY SCOTT BARNARD

HAL•LEONARD®
CORPORATION
7777 W. BLUEMOUND RD. P.O. BOX 13819
MILWAUKEE, WISCONSIN 53213

Preface vii

PART I · CORE TECHNIQUE

1. Left-hand Finger Patterns 1 2
2. Left-hand Finger Patterns 2 4
3. Left-hand Finger Patterns 3 6
4. Left-hand Finger Patterns 4 8
5. Left-hand Finger Patterns 5 10
6. Left-hand Finger Patterns 6 12
7. Left-hand Finger Patterns 7 14
8. Left-hand Finger Patterns 8 16
9. Pull-offs & Hammer-ons 18
10. Pull-offs & Hammer-ons (performance) 20
11. String Crossing 22
12. String Crossing (performance) 23
13. Large Position Changes 25

PART II · HARMONIC TECHNIQUE

14. Root Notes 28
15. 3rds and 7ths 29
16. High Fills with 3rds and 7ths 30
17. Major 9ths 31
18. Major Arpeggios 33
19. Dominant Seventh Arpeggios 34
20. Augmented 7th Arpeggios 35
21. Major/Dominant Seventh/Augmented Arpeggios (performance) 36
22. Minor Arpeggios 38
23. Diminished Arpeggios 39
24. Minor/Diminished Arpeggios (performance) 41
25. Major Scales 43
26. Minor Scales 46
27. Major Pentatonic Scales 48
28. Minor Pentatonic Scales 49
29. Chromatic Scales 50
30. Whole Tone Scales 51
31. Blues Scales 52
32. Scales (performance) 56
33. Guide Tones 57
34. Blues Sequence 59
35. Blues Sequence (performance) 61
36. Minor Blues 62
37. Minor Blues (performance) 63

38. Tritone Substitution Within a ii7–V7–I 64

39. Advancing the Harmony (ii Chord) 66

PART III · ADVANCED STUDY

40. Same Notes, Different Places 68

41. First-finger Barre Across Two Strings 70

42. First-finger Barre Across Three Strings 70

43. First- and Third-finger Barres 71

44. Chords on the Bass 72

45. Chords on the Bass (performance) 75

46. Playing in Octaves 77

47. Rakes 78

48. Slides – Short and Fast 80

49. Slides – Long and Over Multiple Strings 81

50. Left-hand Damping 83

51. Right-hand Damping 84

52. Right Hand as a Volume Pedal 85

53. Left-hand Mute 86

54. Left-hand Mute with a Rake (performance) 87

55. Slap – Thumb Only 88

56. Slap – Drum Loop 89

57. Slap (performance) 91

58. Articulation – Staccato 92

59. Articulation – Tenuto and Staccato (performance) 93

60. Articulation (performance) 94

61. Fast Control 95

62. Fast Control – String Crossing 97

63. Fast Control (performance) 99

64. Rhythm – Soca 100

65. Rhythm – Latin 101

66. Rhythm – Latin (performance) 102

67. Rhythm (performance) 104

68. Sul Tasto 106

69. Sul Tasto (performance) 107

70. Palm Muting 108

71. Palm Muting (performance) 109

72. Harmonics – Natural 110

73. Harmonics – Artificial 112

74. Harmonics – Artificial (performance) 113

75. Drop D Tuning (performance) 115

About the Author 117

PREFACE

This book contains 75 carefully designed exercises and melodies that will challenge you in a fun and musical way. It will touch on various genres, harmony, and musicality in an interesting and methodical approach. Generally, there are one to two exercises given on a topic followed by a "performance" version. However, there are some topics (such as the LH Finger Patterns) that exist solely as fingering exercises. The tempos are given as a guide only, and you should practice the exercises at a speed that allows you to get the most out of the exercises. Suggested fingerings and positions (Roman numerals between the notation and tab staves) are also given.

PART I
CORE TECHNIQUE

1. Left-hand Finger Patterns 1

These first six exercises should all be played legato, using all four left hand fingers. The idea is to always "assign" one finger to one fret. Try to get a good even tone throughout. To eliminate fret buzz, ensure that you place your fingers near the fret wire (rather than on the wire or in the middle of the fret). These exercises are demanding, so if your hand tires, take a rest, and don't overdo it.

2. Left-hand Finger Patterns 2
This exercise will help the change from one finger to another.

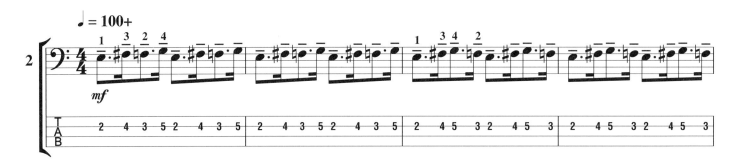

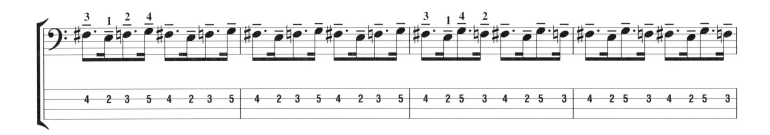

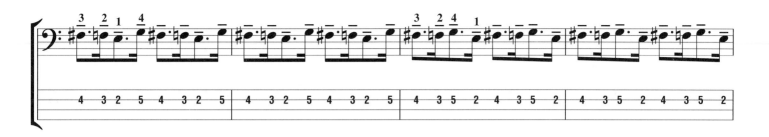

3. Left-hand Finger Patterns 3

This exercise is, rhythmically speaking, the reverse of exercise 2 and on a thicker string, so it may be a little trickier.

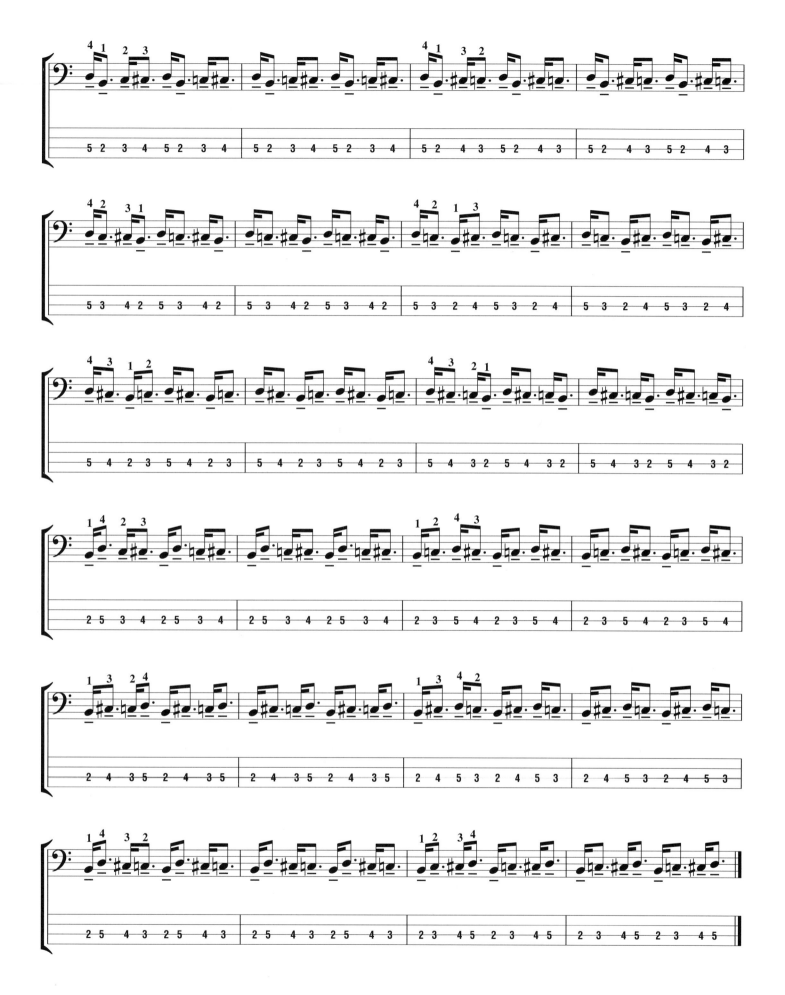

4. Left-hand Finger Patterns 4

Although this exercise will produce some strange arpeggios at times, try to play it with beauty, ensuring long, legato notes. Again, rest whenever necessary.

5. Left-hand Finger Patterns 5

This exercise is the reverse of exercise 4; in other words, we're descending through the strings instead of ascending.

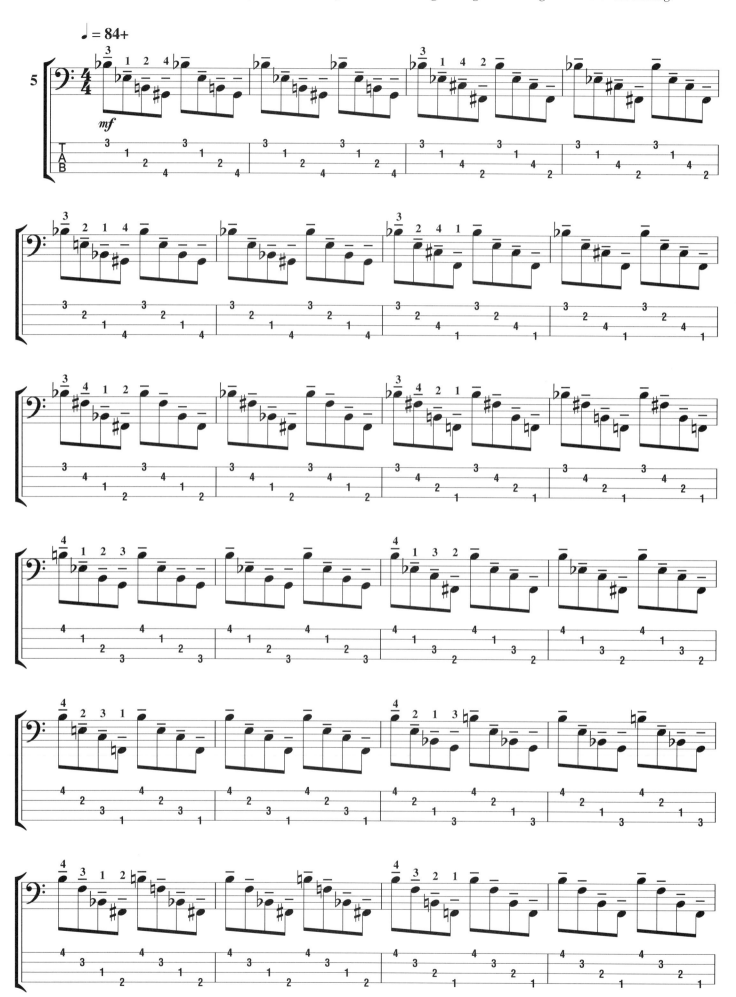

6. Left-hand Finger Patterns 6
This exercise is a great work out for both left-and right-hand fingers.

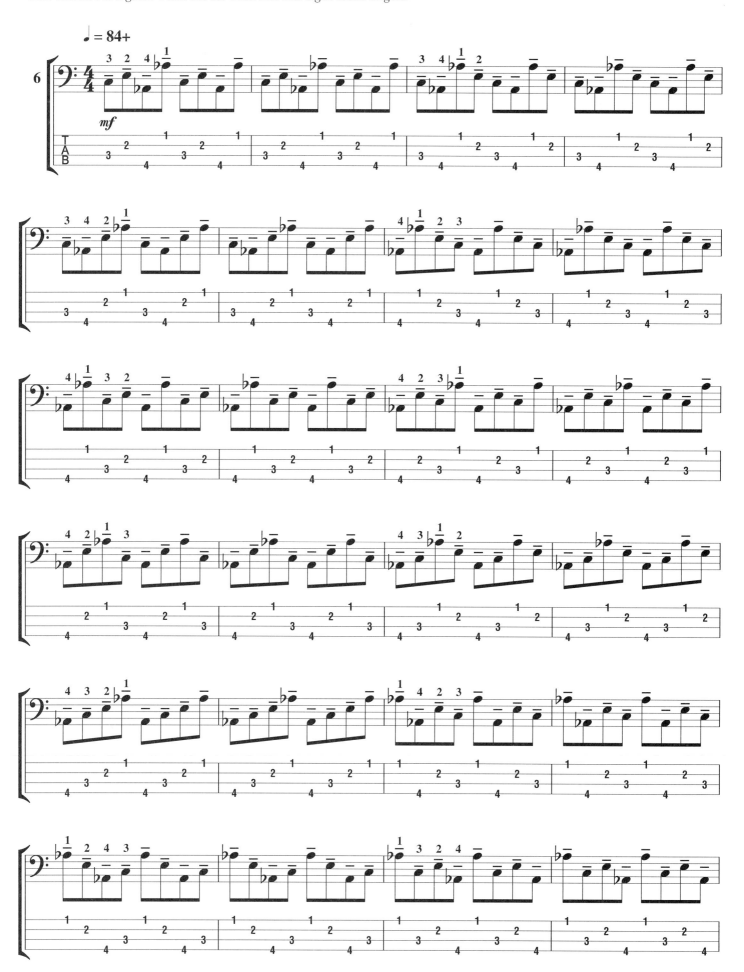

7. Left-hand Finger Patterns 7

In this exercise, you concentrate on just two strings. Notice that you have two different articulations on the same string.

8. Left-hand Finger Patterns 8

This exercise pushes things a little further with staccatos on one string and tenutos on another.

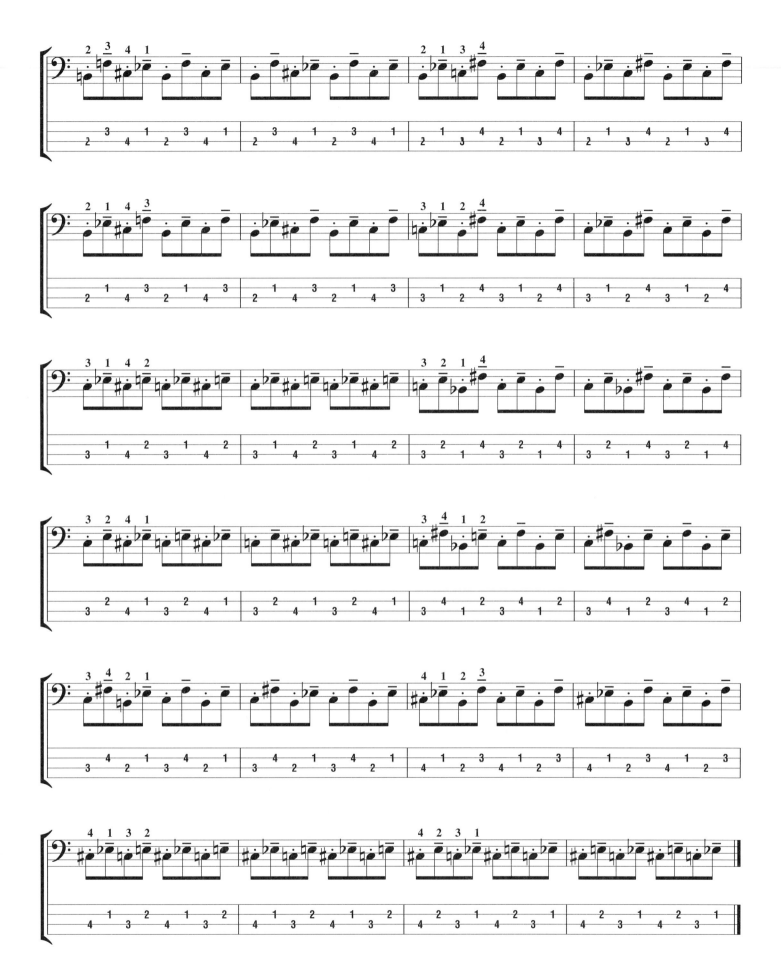

9. Pull-offs & Hammer-ons

Play this one loudly, as you will need to get the string to vibrate as you carry out the hammer-ons and pull-offs. Occasionally, you'll have some position changes during the middle of the slur. With the pull-offs, you will get a better result if you pull the finger towards the floor, rather than just lifting it up. In the second example, there are some pretty serious stretches, so take breaks when you need to.

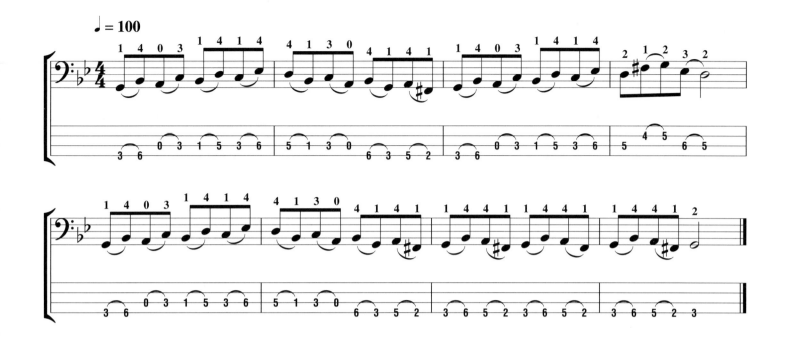

10. Pull-offs & Hammer-ons (performance)

There are many position changes in this one. If you're not sure of some of the notes, the tab can help you.

11. String Crossing

This exercise features a simple disco-style groove over a minor blues chord sequence, with intervals of octaves and 7ths. Use your middle and index fingers and concentrate on the upper notes as a melodic line.

12. String Crossing (performance)

In this exercise, you have many elements that you'll come across in a disco track. At letter A, there's a right-hand fingering suggestion where you can use your thumb as well as index and middle fingers (p – i – m). This will make the rhythm much easier to play, but you'll need to work on getting the thumb stroke to sound full. At letter B, concentrate on the note after the end of each slide (rather than the start of the slide). At letter C, you could try a barre with the first finger to make this line more manageable.

13. Large Position Changes

This exercise deals with octave jumps on the same string. Don't worry if you can't read the higher notes (they are all an octave higher than the note that precedes it). Watch your left hand closely as you practice this one. After several times through, try the whole exercise without looking at your left hand at all.

PART II
HARMONIC TECHNIQUE

14. Root Notes

Firstly, play this exercise without any articulations. You should find that the first few bars sound fine and outline the chords well. After that, the line jumps around, rarely placing the root of a chord on a strong beat of the bar. The second time you play through it, emphasize the root notes by playing them slightly longer and with a slight accent. This should help make sense of the underlying harmony. In general, this is a good practice to adopt when playing the bass.

15. 3rds and 7ths

Here are some Seventh chords with a finger shape that highlights the 3rds and 7ths. If you have the 3rd of the chord on top, the 7th will be on bottom, and vice versa. You can use this shape as a basis for a fill on a dominant 7th chord (as shown in exercise 16). You may find it helpful to sing the root note while you play this exercise.

16. High Fills with 3rds and 7ths

Here are some simple examples of how to use the 3rd/7th shapes as fills.

17. Major 9th

There are many famous bass lines that are based on the interval of a major 9th (or which outline that chord). It's a good way to create a line that stays on one chord for a period of time while maintaining interest. Here are a few examples within a sequence.

18. Major Arpeggios

Arpeggios make up a large proportion of bass lines, but as chord sequences are often repetitive, it's useful to be able to vary how you use them. This may include starting on different notes of the triad and moving in different directions, etc. Here's an exercise purely made from the arpeggios of C, F, and G major.

19. Dominant Seventh Arpeggios

This exercise looks at the dominant seventh chord as an arpeggio.

20. Augmented 7th Arpeggios

The augmented chord, or arpeggio, is similar to the major chord but with a raised 5th. For example, a C augmented chord would contain the notes C, E, and G♯ (a triad built up of all major 3rds). The chord symbol for this is "aug," "+," "+5," or "♯5," and it's often used as a passing chord.

21. Major/Dominant Seventh/Augmented Arpeggios (performance)

This exercise contains major, dominant seventh, and augmented arpeggios in various inversions.

22. Minor Arpeggios

Here are some minor arpeggio patterns with which to get familiar.

23. Diminished Arpeggios

Diminished seventh chords or arpeggios are based on consecutive minor 3rds: root, ♭3rd, ♭5th, dim 7th (often spelled enharmonically as a major 6th). Though the suffix "dim" or "°" technically denotes a diminished *triad* (root–♭3rd–♭5th), the chord symbol for a diminished seventh chord will sometimes appear as that as well. Its proper name, however, includes a "7" at the end—e.g., C°7 or Cdim7. Notice the "crab-like" pattern this arpeggio shape creates with your left hand.

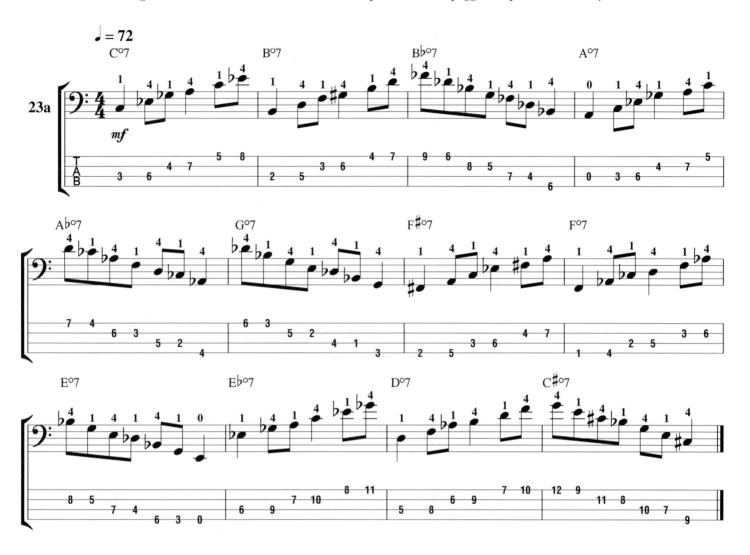

Half diminished seventh chords are similar, except the dim 7th is replaced with a ♭7th. These chords are denoted with a line through the circle (ø) or as a minor seventh chord with a ♭5th—e.g., Cø7 or Cm7♭5.

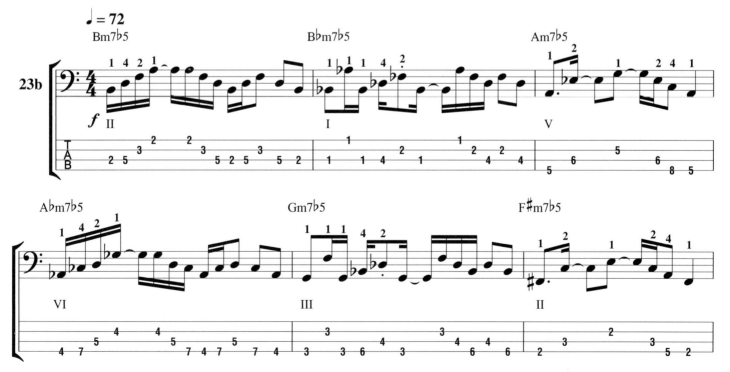

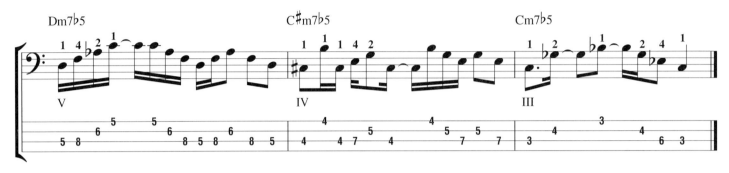

24. Minor/Diminished Arpeggios (performance)

This exercise covers minor and diminished arpeggios. Work out your own fingerings for these based on the previous exercises. The tab may also prove useful if you're unsure.

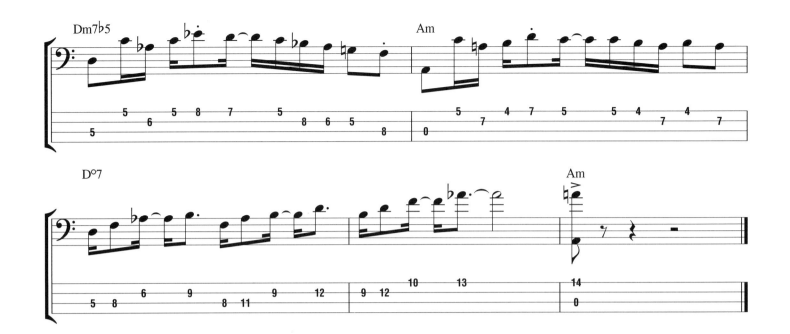

25. Major Scales

These exercises show various major scale patterns in the key of C. You should extend them by playing them in every key. (The positions are obviously only valid for this key.)

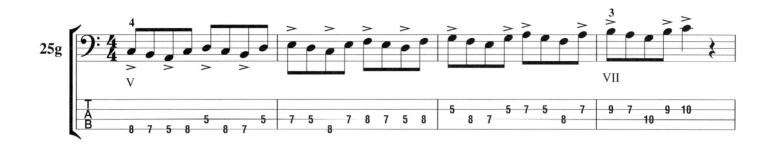

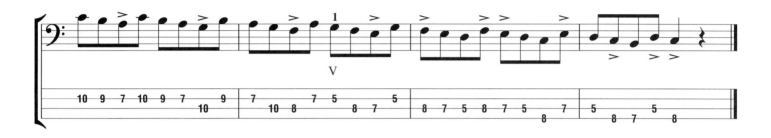

26. Minor Scales

Here are some exercises that look at the three different types of minor scales. There are various ways in which to handle the position changes; here are some of the most straightforward. Try them in a few different keys.

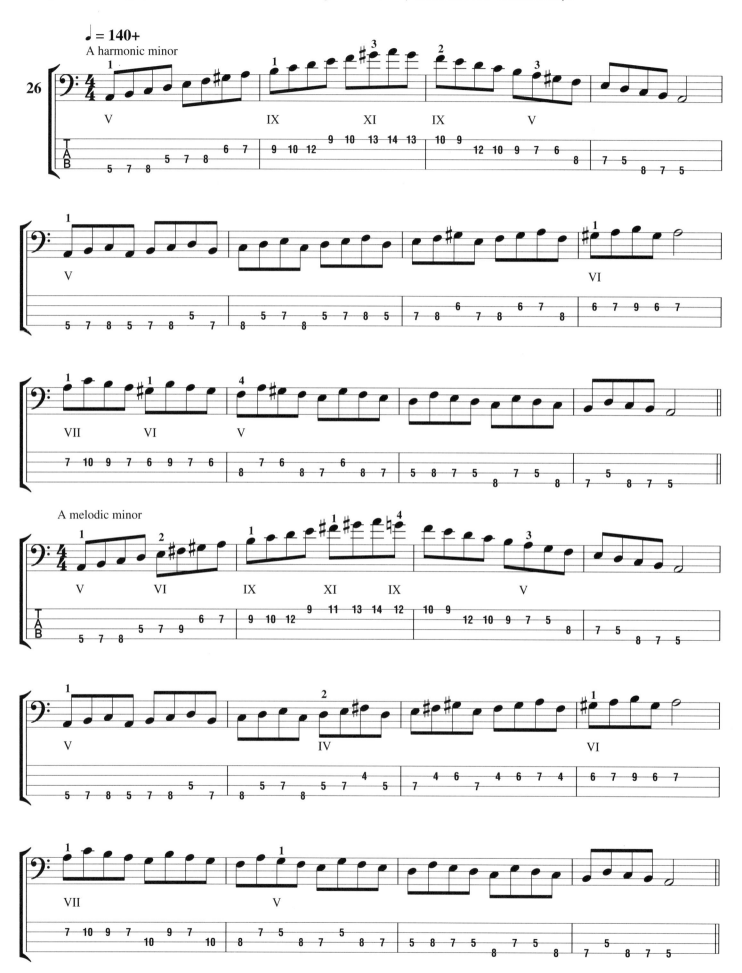

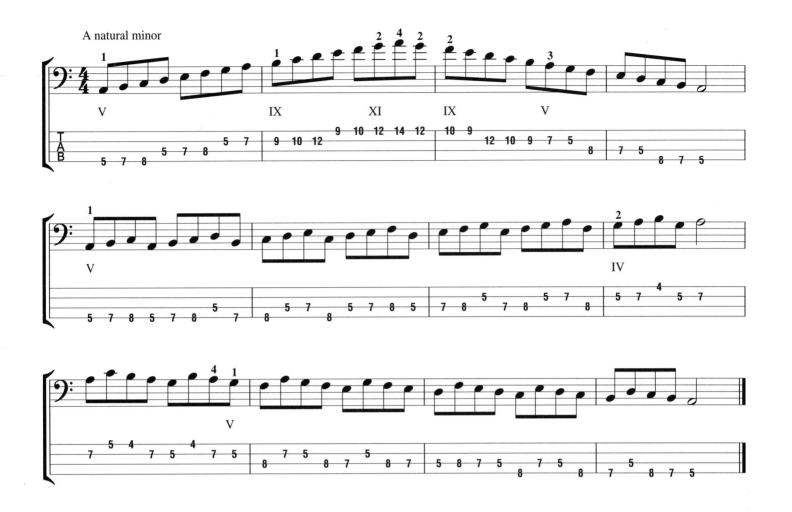

27. Major Pentatonic Scales

Major pentatonic scales use five degrees taken from the major scale: the root, 2nd, 3rd, 5th, and 6th.

28. Minor Pentatonic Scales

Minor pentatonic scales use five degrees taken from the natural minor scale: the root, ♭3rd, 4th, 5th, and ♭7th.

29. Chromatic Scales

The chromatic scale has a memorable pattern. When you cross to a higher string, move your hand position down one fret; when crossing to a lower string, move your hand position up one fret. Exercises 29b and 29c have a slight variation in which there is a position change on each string before continuing with the pattern. I have bracketed where notes are to be played on one string.

30. Whole Tone Scales

There are really only two whole tone scales: one starting on C (C–D–E–F#–G#–A#), and the other on C# (C#–D#–F–G–A–B). All other whole tone scales will start from a point within one of these scales.

31. Blues Scales

The blues scale comprises the root, ♭3rd, 4th, ♭5th, natural 5th, and ♭7th. The ♭3rd, ♭5th, and ♭7th are known as "blue" notes and give the scale its bluesy quality. Here it is in every key, with a sample bluesy line following each. (Note that some of the ♭5ths have been written enharmonically, as ♯4ths, for ease of reading.)

32. Scales (performance)

Try to spot all the scale patterns throughout this exercise.

33. Guide Tones

As the bass player, you generally want a good helping of root notes in a bass part, but it's also good to be aware of the guide tones. Guide tones are the "essence" of a chord. They are usually the 3rds and 7ths and are useful when improvising or constructing a bass line.

Exercise 33a shows a chord sequence with the root, 3rds, and 7ths of each chord. Exercise 33b shows how to navigate these chords by moving to the nearest guide tone (using the notes D, C, C, B♭, A♯, G♯, and G♮). Exercise 33c shows how you might approach a solo over this sequence (the guide tones are shown here as circle notes.)

34. Blues Sequence

The 12-bar blues sequence often crops up in rock and roll, jazz, and pop tunes. There are some slight differences between them, however, with the jazz versions usually containing more substituted chords. Exercise 34a shows a very simple rock and roll line in A, while exercise 34b demonstrates some variations to try. Exercise 34c shows a typical jazz blues in A, with added chords, and 34d is the same sequence transposed to F with some variations.

35. Blues Sequence (performance)

Here are a couple choruses of a jazz blues in G. The first chorus is the head, and the second is an improvisation. Note how parts of the head are used and/or transformed for the solo section. Also try to spot where the guide tones have be used in both sections.

36. Minor Blues

Here is a very simple minor blues in A minor. Chords are often made into minor 7th chords, and the V chord may or may not be major (in this case, it is: E major). Minor pentatonic scales can work well for bass lines and improvisation.

37. Minor Blues (performance)

This minor blues is a little more complex than the previous one. All chords have been made into 7th chords. Here are the variations:

- Bar 2 is a iv chord (Dm7)
- Bar 4 is a major (dominant, actually) version of the I chord (A7)
- Bar 9 is a ♭VI chord (F7)
- Bar 10 is a V chord (E7)
- Bar 12 is a V chord (E7)

38. Tritone Substitution Within a ii7–V7–I

In a chord sequence, you may come across a ii7–V7–I progression (often at the end of a section or sometimes as a temporary modulation). The V7 chord can be been replaced with a ♭II7 chord for an altered sound. This is called a *tritone substitution*, as the new chord is a tritone away from the original. This works well because both chords (V7 and ♭II7) contain the same 3rds and 7ths—albeit that they are inverted. In other words, the 3rd of the V chord is the ♭7th of the ♭II chord, whereas the 3rd of the ♭II chord is the ♭7th of the V chord.

In C major, a ii7–V7–I progression would be Dm7–G7–C. With the tritone sub method, this could become Dm7–D♭7–C. Here are some ii7–V7–I progressions followed by a version with a tritone substitution.

Tritone substitutions sound great if used sparingly and within the correct context. A jazz or funk tune would be appropriate, but you may get a few frowns if you try it in a straight-ahead pop setting.

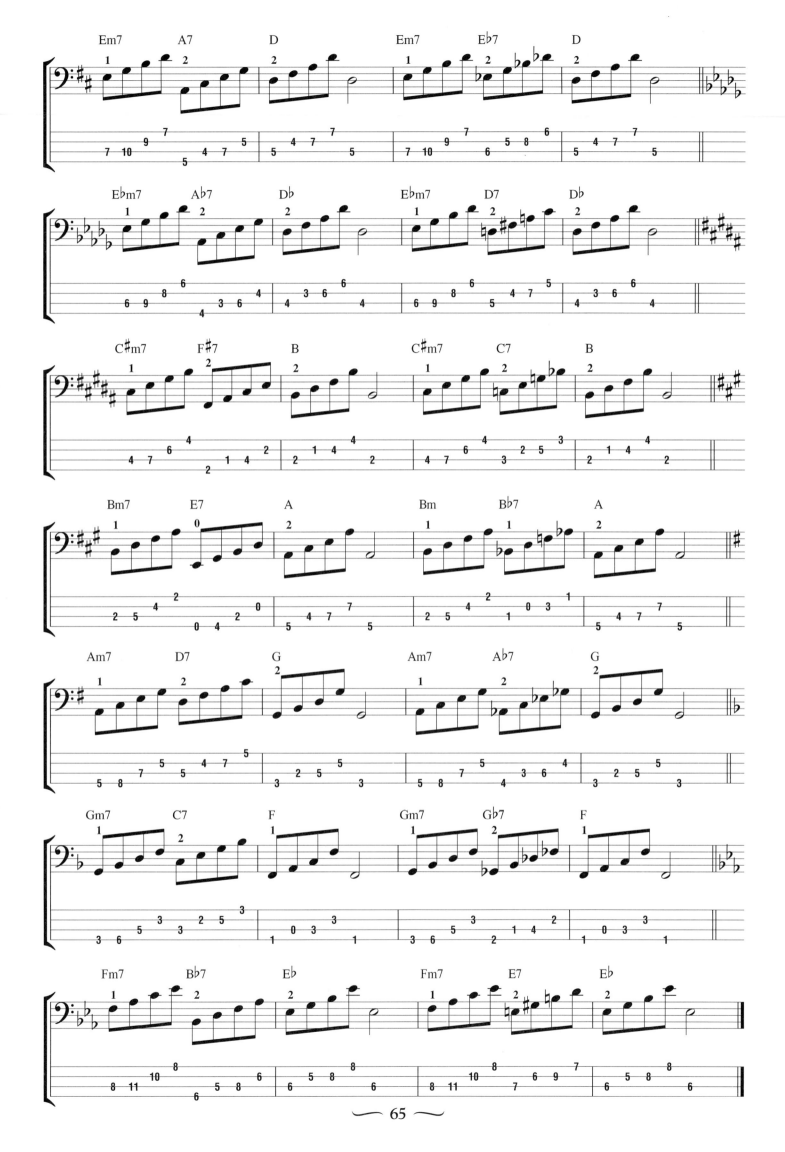

39. Advancing the Harmony (ii Chord)

With minor chords, it is not generally recommended to use a tritone substitution. However, there is something else that you can do as the bass player. When you see a ii–V–I progression, you can "advance" the harmony by playing the V chord early (where chord ii would normally be). So, instead of the chords Gm7–C7–F (exercise 39a), you will produce Gm7/C–C7–F (exercise 39b). (The Gm7/C effectively results in the chord of C11.)

Occasionally, you could also substitute the V chord, as in exercise 38, thus transforming Gm7–C7–F into Gm7/C–Gb7–F (exercise 39c). Like the tritone sub, use this idea sparingly to give it maximum effect. Here, the chords have been written as arpeggios so that you get an idea of what the harmony sounds like. In an actual playing situation, however, you would normally just play the root notes (C–C–F or C–Gb–F).

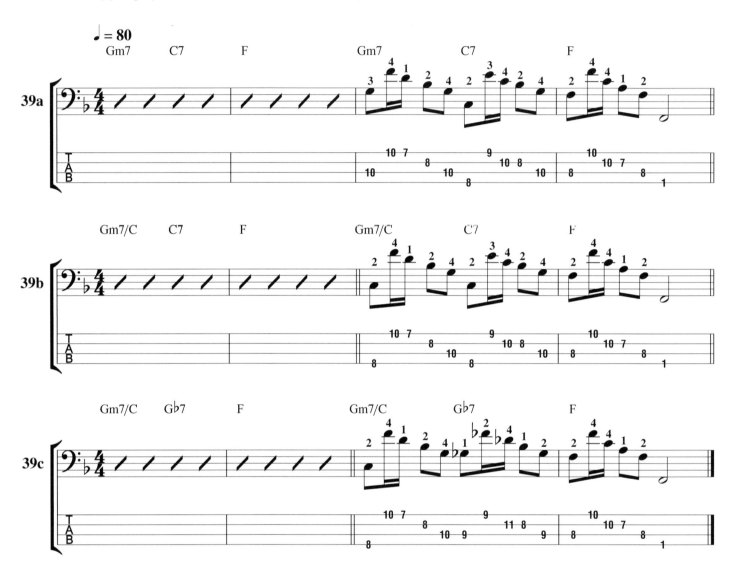

PART III
ADVANCED STUDY

40. Same Notes, Different Places

Knowing all spots on the neck where a note can be played will help you to avoid unnecessary position changes. Try these exercises. The circled numbers indicate which string to play (we'll just go up to the 18th fret here).

   Exercise 40b looks at small phrases played in different places on the neck as well as in different octaves (the circled numbers indicate the starting string).

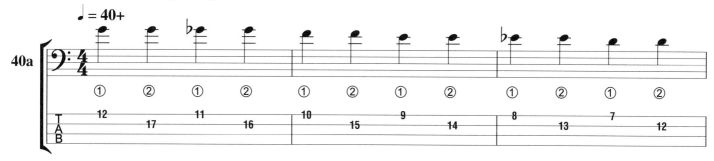

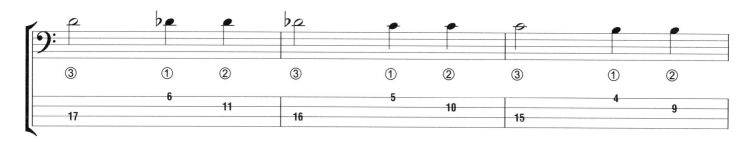

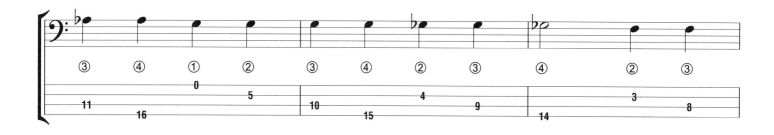

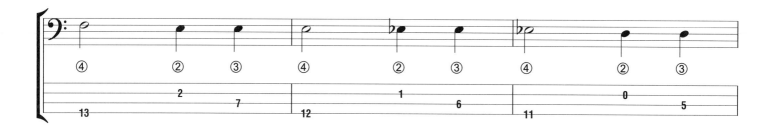

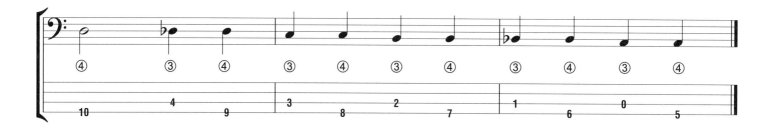

41. First-finger Barre Across Two Strings

You can use your left index finger to barre across several strings. This can be a useful technique to keep finger movement to a minimum. In exercise 41, barre with your index finger across the G and D strings.

42. First-finger Barre Across Three Strings

In this exercise, barre across the G, D, and A strings. You may notice that the final few measures are derived from an F minor pentatonic scale.

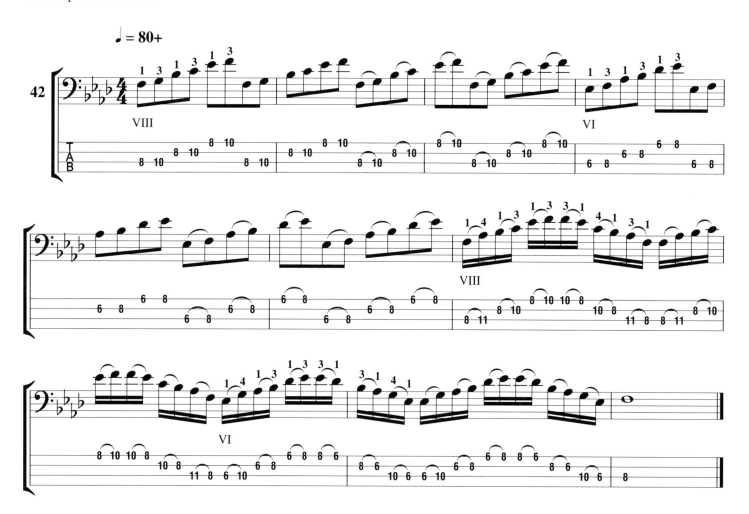

43. First- and Third-finger Barres

This exercise looks at using two barres: one with the first finger and one with the third, both on the top two strings. The first-finger barre should be in place throughout. The third-finger barre should be down wherever possible and "seesaw" at other times. For instance, in bar 4, start with both barres in place; then after the D has been played, lift the barre slightly to allow the C to sound. The third-finger should still be in place for the A note on string 2, but then remove it to play the G.

44. Chords on the Bass

The bass usually only plays one note at a time, but occasionally it can be interesting to include a two- or three-note chord. You'll notice that they sound better the higher up the neck you go.

Exercise 44a produces simple major/minor shapes, while 44b deals with major/minor sevenths. 44c looks at major and minor 3rds, and 44d is similar but with an additional root note. 44e shows how to play three-note seventh chords. The strings to use are marked at the start of each exercise.

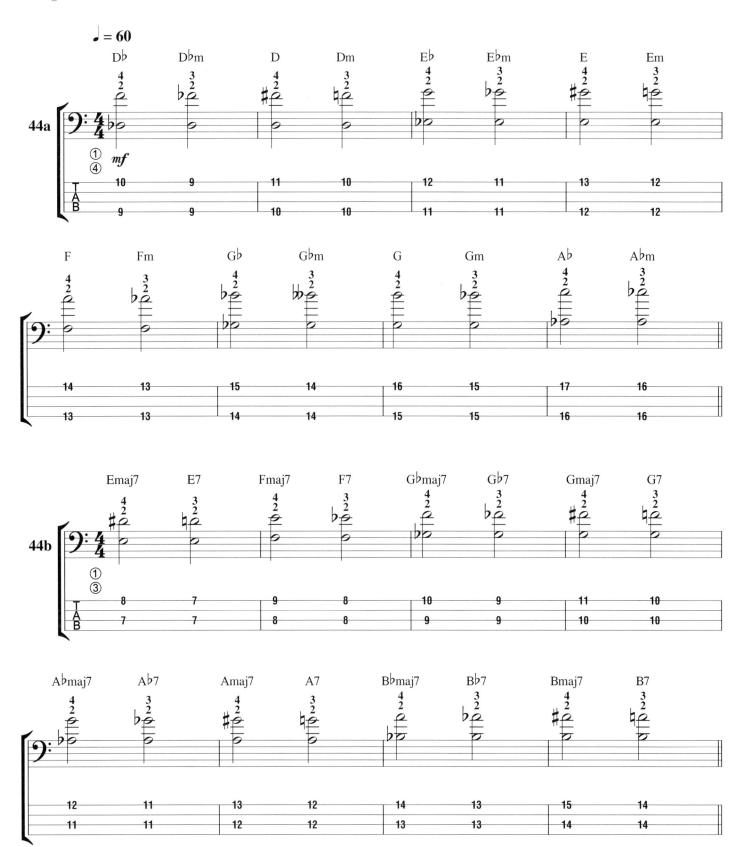

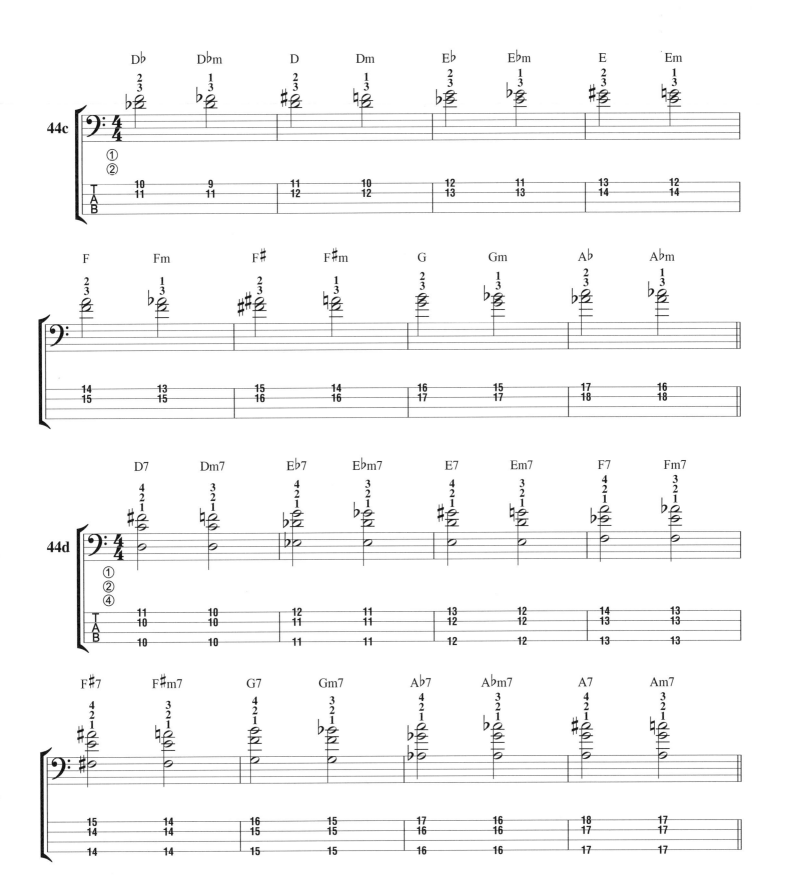

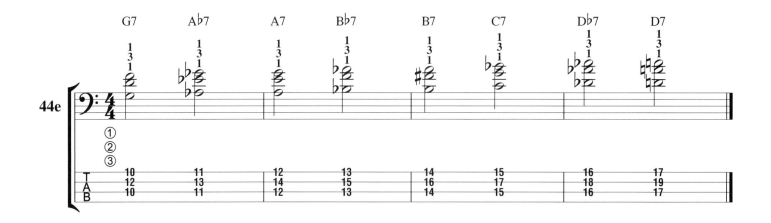

45. Chords on the Bass (performance)

Here are some sequences that you might find useful.

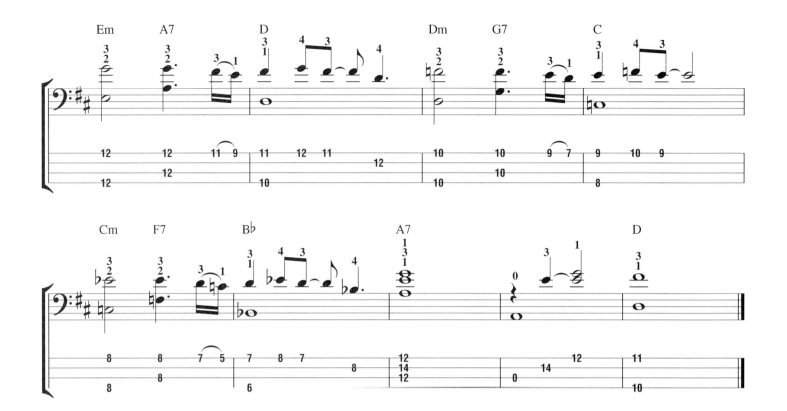

46. Playing in Octaves

Another way to play two notes on the bass is in octaves. This can add a nice full tone to part of a bass line. You can try adding in some slides, too. Use the same hand shape for all these notes, concentrating on where your first finger will end up. Bear in mind that, as you go higher, the distance between your first and fourth fingers reduces.

47. Rakes

Rakes are a way of using the same right-hand finger to quickly move from a higher string to a lower string. Make sure that they are strictly rhythmical—use a metronome.

Exercise 47a looks at two- and three-string rakes, while exercise 47b deals with four-string rakes. Both exercises include notes after the rakes, so that they are more useful to you when incorporating them in your playing.

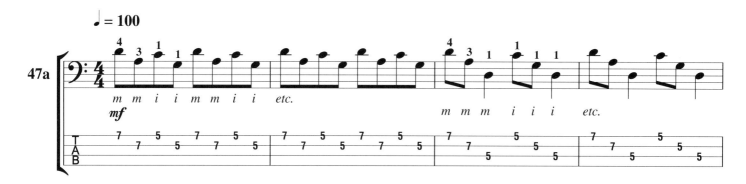

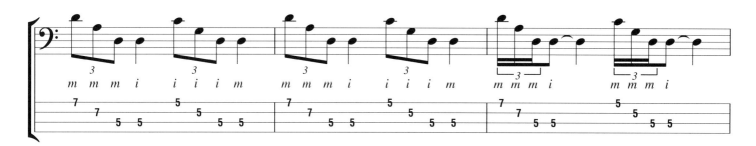

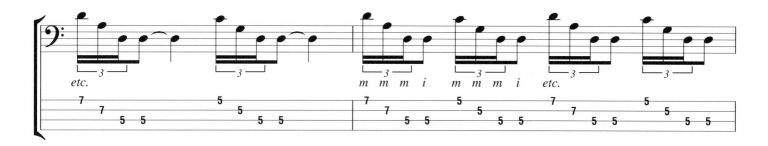

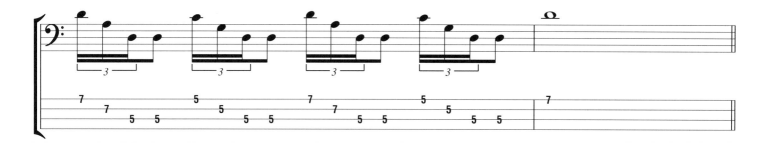

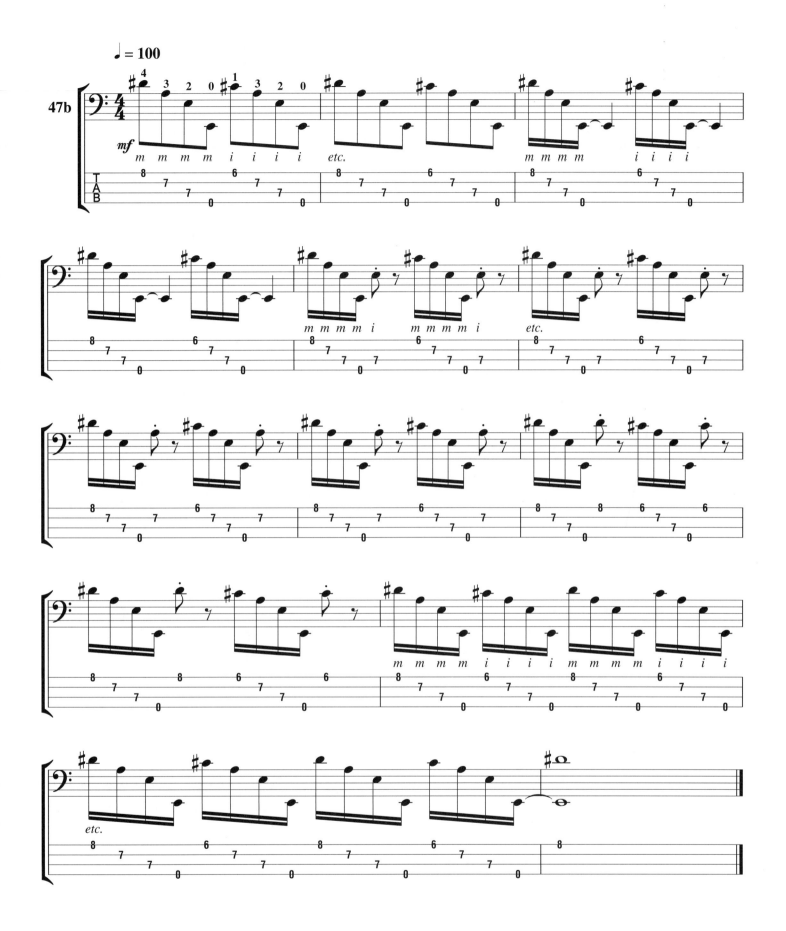

48. Slides – Short and Fast

Here's an exercise to help you to master the slide. Focus on where you want your first finger to end up and use a metronome. Make the distinction between the 16th-note slides and the little scoops, which should be much faster and on the beat.

49. Slides – Long and Over Multiple Strings

Exercise 49 is a slow blues in A. The second half of this exercise (from bar 13 on) introduces some slides. I wouldn't recommend adding this many in a live situation! There is a three-string slide at the end of bar 12. To play this, start at approximately the pitch given on the first string and then move your left hand down the neck while catching a slide on the second and then third strings. The one in bar 20 is similar, except it's on the second, third, and fourth strings. Enjoy!

50. Left-hand Damping

Left-hand damping is important for a variety of reasons. Firstly, you can stop any unwanted overtones from other strings by resting a finger that you're not using on them. For example, play this first exercise. If you have any unwanted resonance, in this case, it is most likely to be coming from the G string. Play it again, but this time rest your first finger across the strings (around the first fret) to stop them vibrating in sympathy.

The second important reason to use left-hand damping is to control the length of notes. Play exercise 50b with a metronome. To get a clear silence on the rest, you can try one of two things: slightly release the pressure on your first finger—that should be enough to stop the string from vibrating—or, introduce the rest of your left-hand fingers on the string to stop it from vibrating. Having control over your notes lengths in this way greatly adds to your feel.

Once you're comfortable with both methods, try exercise 50c. Use the string-release method to produce a staccato; do not use any open strings. Do not damp the string with the right hand. If you find it tricky to resist, just play the exercise with one right hand finger.

51. Right-hand Damping

You can also affect your note lengths with right-hand damping. Try exercise 51. After each index finger stroke, stop the string from vibrating by placing your right hand middle finger on the string and vice versa. Do not use any left-hand damping techniques for this exercise.

52. Right Hand as a Volume Pedal

This next exercise is fairly unusual. If you haven't got a volume pedal, or you just want to have some added control over the volume of a note, you can carry a decrease in volume by placing a right hand finger on the vibrating string somewhere near, or on, the bridge. It won't have much effect on the bridge, but as you slowly slide your finger away from the bridge, it will affect the string's ability to vibrate. You can produce a diminuendo to complete rest once you have full control of this technique. You can also make more sudden decreases in volume. Try the following exercise with a metronome.

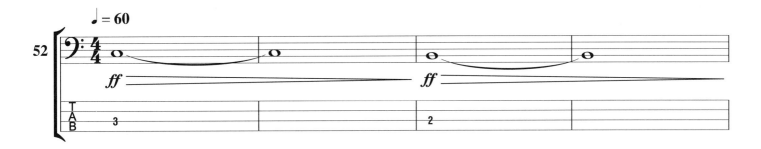

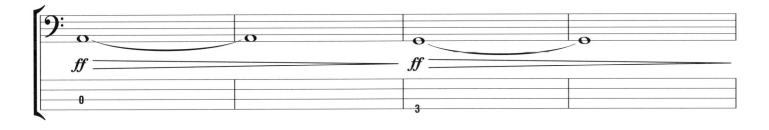

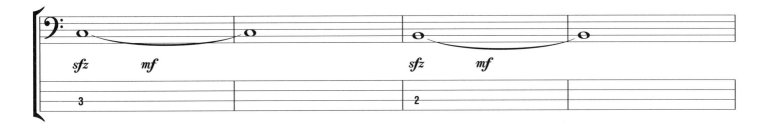

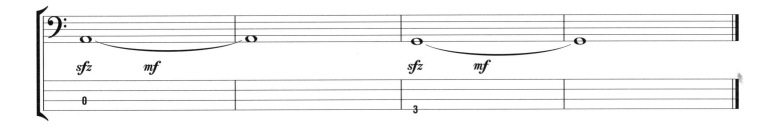

53. Left-hand Mute

The left-hand mute uses the techniques of left-hand damping while striking the string in the normal way with the right hand. This produces a sound of indeterminate pitch and can add a certain funkiness to a bass line. Try using both left-hand damping techniques on this exercise.

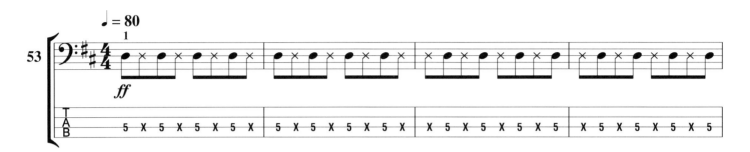

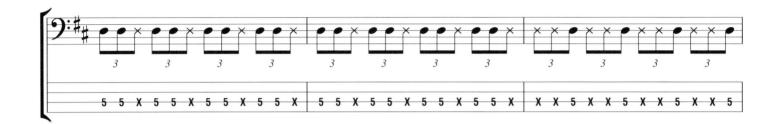

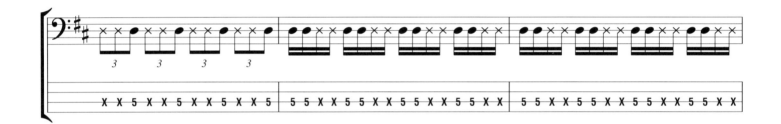

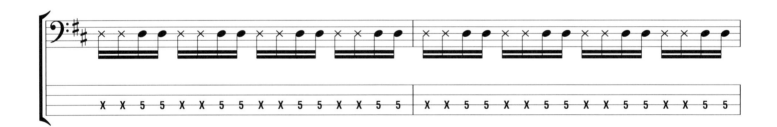

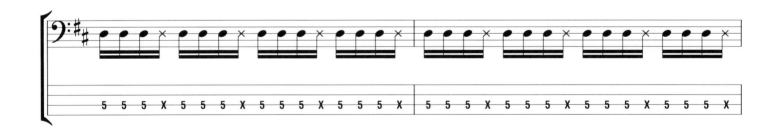

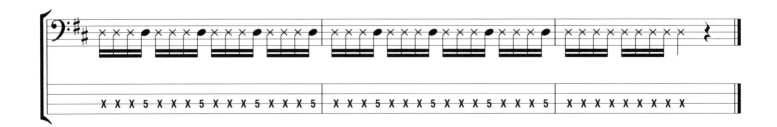

54. Left-hand Mute with a Rake (performance)

A nice effect is to play a muted, raked figure. In this exercise, I would suggest the "note release" left-hand technique for the triplet rakes and the "add additional fingers" left-hand technique for the 16th-note mutes.

55. Slap – Thumb Only

To get a good slap sound, use new strings (they will have more "bounce" and presence) and add some more bass into your sound by adjusting your tone controls. Also make sure that you work solely on the thumb stroke first so that you are getting a full sound. "S" indicates a "slapped" note. Use a metronome!

56. Slap – Drum Loop

Once your thumb stroke is sounding good, add in the pulled, or popped, notes. These exercises are like drum grooves, where the slapped thumb will act as the bass drum, and the pulls act as the snare. "P" indicates a "pulled" note. Use a metronome.

57. Slap (performance)

You will often find many other techniques used simultaneously with slap playing, such as muted notes (both slapped and pulled), slides, falls, hammer-ons, and pull-offs. All of these are represented in this next example. Use a metronome.

58. Articulation – Staccato

This exercise uses right-hand damping (see exercise 51) to produce the staccato notes. Alternate the index and middle fingers on the right hand; after each note is struck, use the next finger to stop the string before it strikes it. In other words, strike the first note with your index finger, stop the string from vibrating with your middle finger, play the second note with your middle finger, and stop it with your index finger, etc.

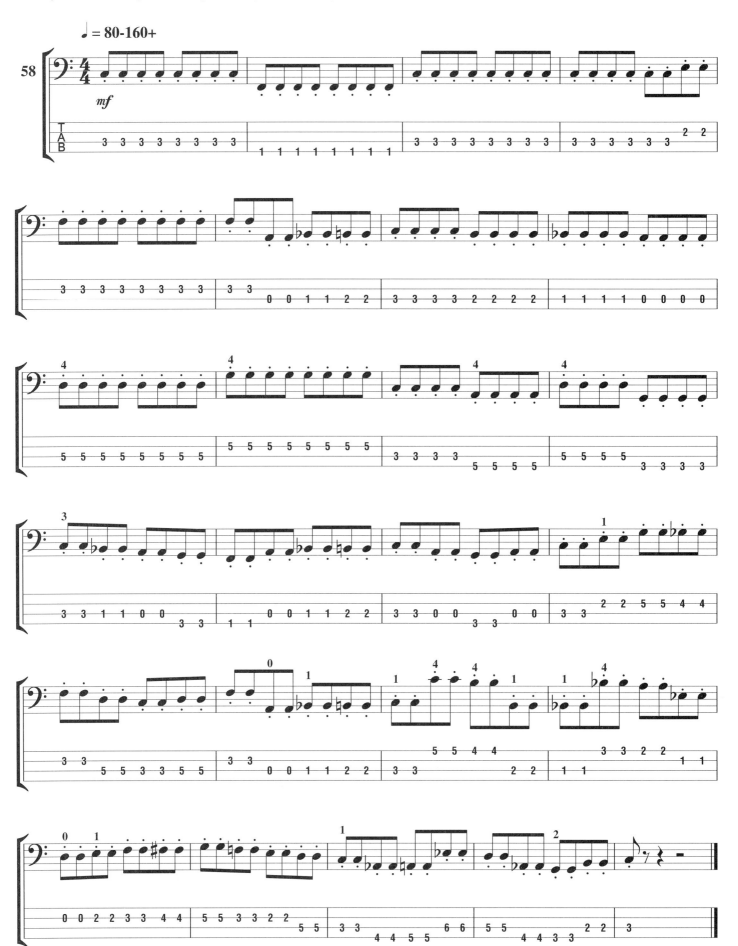

59. Articulation – Tenuto and Staccato (performance)

Make an exaggeration of the tenuto and staccato notes. This exercise is not as easy as it may first appear!

60. Articulation (performance)

For this tune, we'll add some accents into the mix.

61. Fast Control

Many tunes are based on repeated eighth-note patterns, requiring right-hand stamina, evenness of tone, and left-hand precision. Try this exercise to work on these areas.

62. Fast Control – String Crossing

This exercise includes string crossings but also requires right-hand stamina and an even tone on the repeated notes.

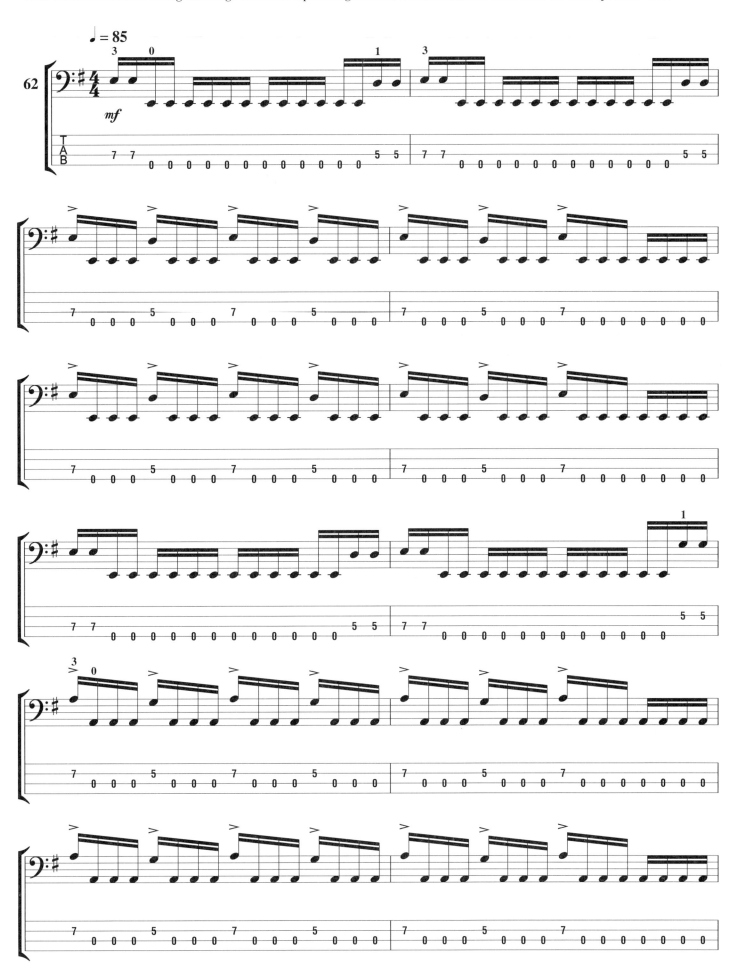

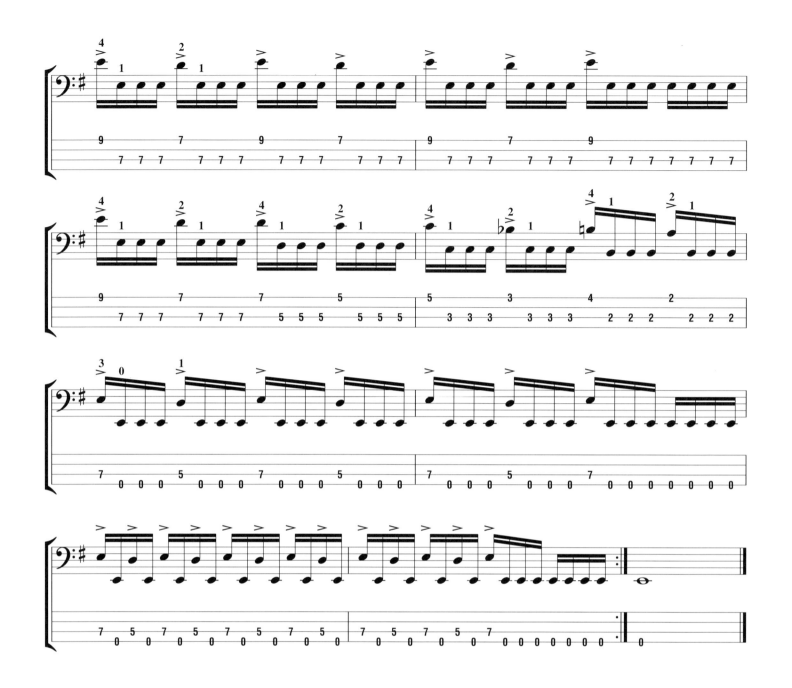

63. Fast Control (performance)

This exercise pivots around just two chords with a funky, rhythmic line. Try to keep the notes fairly short, unless marked otherwise.

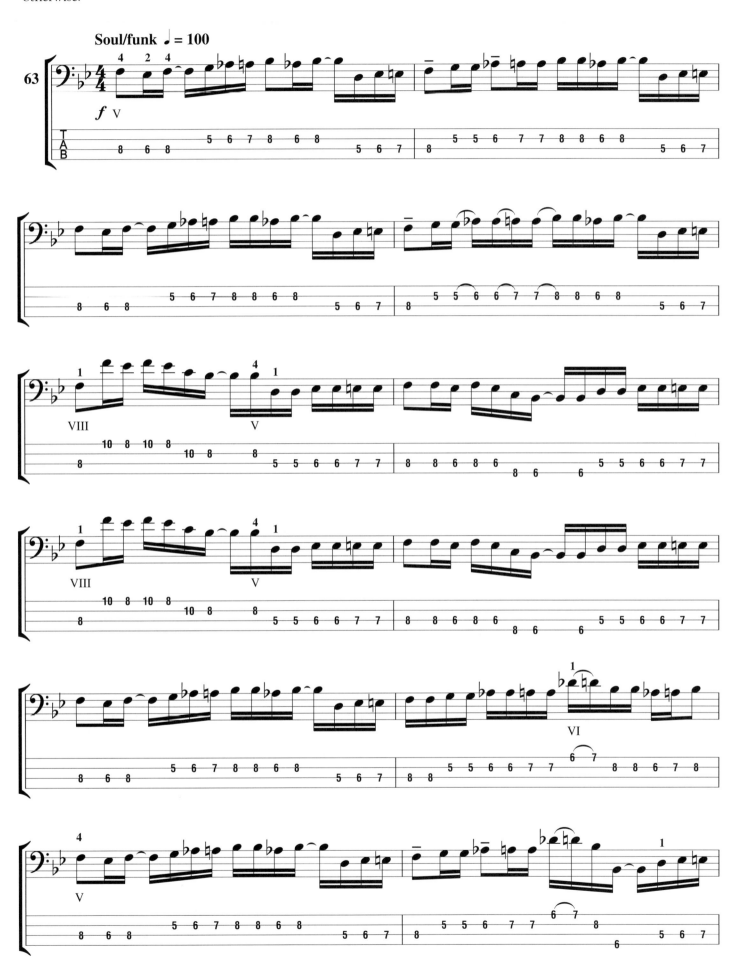

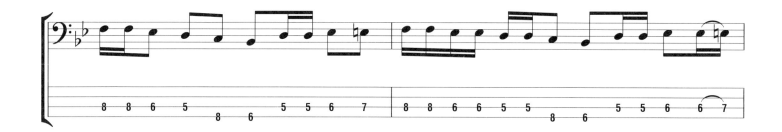

64. Rhythm – Soca

Here's a pattern reminiscent of a Soca tune. Be careful not to lose where you are in the bar, as there aren't any notes to play on beats 1 or 3. Use a metronome.

65. Rhythm – Latin

There are some important rhythms to know when playing any Latin-based music. The rhythmic structure is usually based on a *clave*. These are five-note, repeated patterns. The bass may or may not play these, but it's good to know what other players are going to be doing.

   The first is called a "Son clave" and can be either a group of three notes followed by two or vice versa—known as 3:2 or 2:3 Son claves. The second is a variation of this called a "Rhumba clave," where the third note in the group of three is played later, producing a 3:2 or 2:3 Rhumba clave.

   If the bass is not playing a clave, it is likely that you will be playing a syncopated repeated figure called a "Tumbao." Notice here how each chord is anticipated by one beat. Here are some examples of each. Use a metronome.

66. Rhythm – Latin (performance)

Some of the rhythms from the previous exercise are used in this one. However, some have been altered to reflect what a bass player might do in a live situation. Use a metronome.

67. Rhythm (performance)

This exercise is full of syncopated riffs and figures you'll often come across in pop bass lines. If you follow the correct positions and fingerings, the higher passages become much easier. Use a metronome.

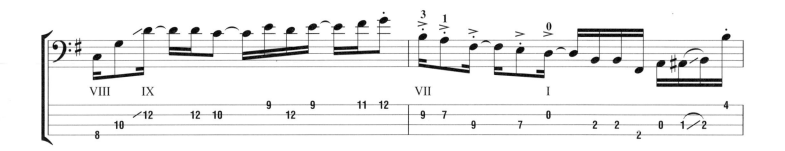

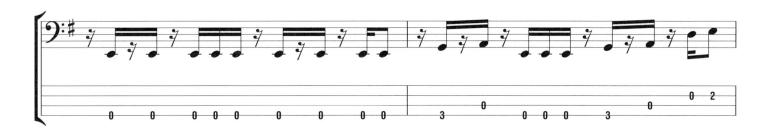

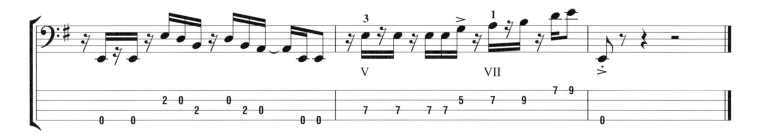

68. Sul Tasto (performance)

The direction "Sul tasto" indicates that your right hand should pluck the strings over the fingerboard. This produces a rich, full sound that can be used on a ballad or when wanting to approximate a double bass or even sub-bass type of sound. Here's an exercise using Sul tasto on a ballad.

69. Sul Tasto (performance)

This next exercise explores some possibilities of using the Sul tasto effect on a pop tune.

70. Palm Muting

Palm putting is a nice effect that can add some color—perhaps for a whole tune or maybe just on a verse or a particular fill, etc. To do this, rest the side of your right palm on the strings, near the bridge. You can alter the amount the strings are muted by moving closer or farther away from the bridge. Usually you would pluck the notes with your right-hand thumb, but experiment with occasionally adding in your index finger for faster passages or lines with string crossings.

71. Palm Muting (performance)

Here is the palm mute being used for some typical reggae rhythms.

72. Harmonics – Natural

Harmonics are a nice feature to add to a phrase, providing it is done sparingly. On each string, you can produce several natural harmonics. Relating to the open string, they produce the following notes:

- **12th fret:** an octave above
- **Seventh fret:** an octave and a 5th above
- **Fifth fret:** Two octaves above
- **Fourth (or ninth) fret:–** Two octaves and a major 3rd above

Here are some exercises using natural harmonics built around major triads. The harmonics are written at pitch and show the fret number of where it is to be produced, along with the string number.

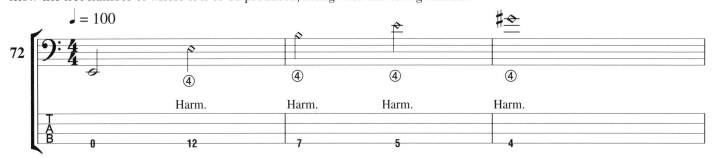

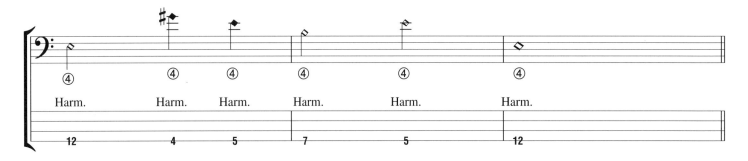

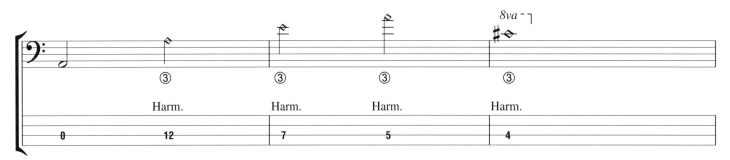

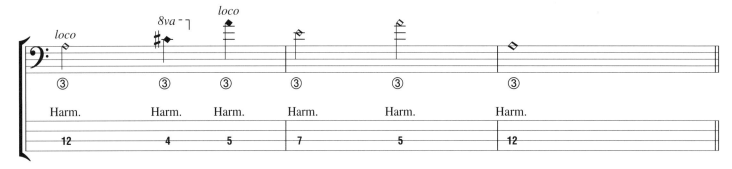

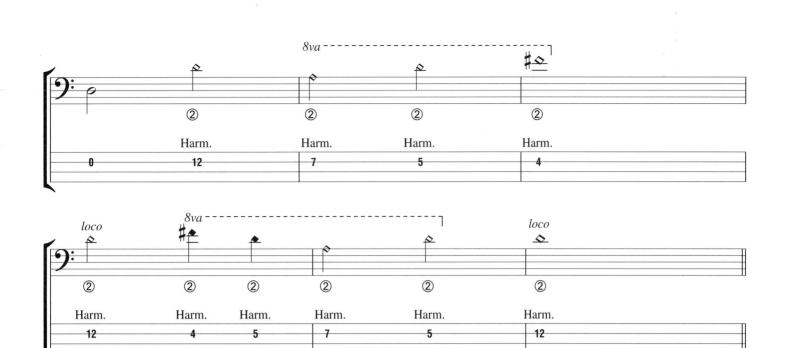
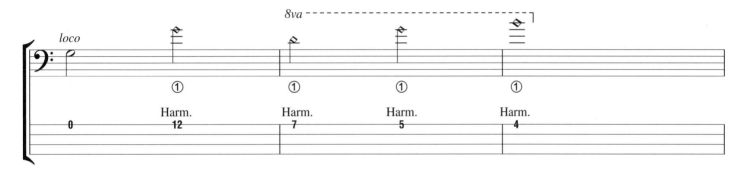
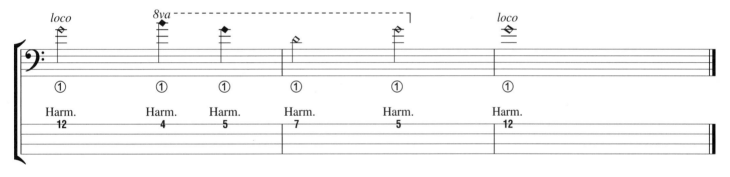

73. Harmonics – Artificial

Artificial harmonics are produced by fretting a note normally with the left hand and then lightly placing your right index finger 12 frets above. You strike the string with the right ring finger. You may find it easier to look at your right hand for this exercise.

74. Harmonics – Artificial (performance)

In this exercise, the first section is to be played as normal, so that you can see how the fingering and position changes work. Then try the second section: It is exactly the same except the upper notes will be played as artificial harmonics, one octave above the written notes.

The last note is tricky, as you need to use your thumb (for the lower note) and produce the harmonic at the same time.

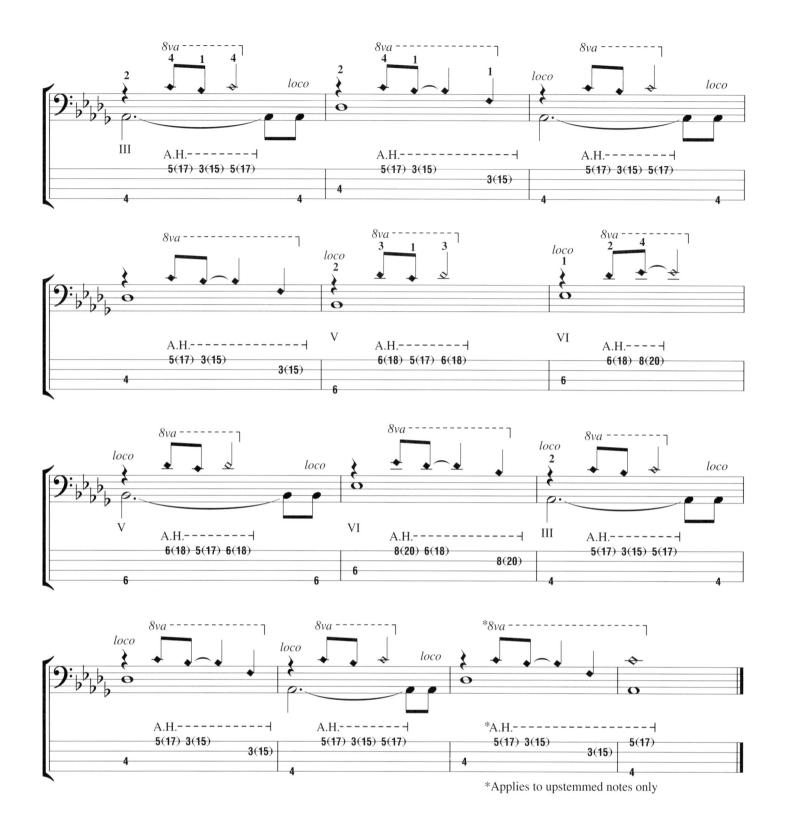

*Applies to upstemmed notes only

75. Drop D Tuning (performance)

If you have a four-string bass, you can detune the E string down a whole step to D (known as drop-D tuning) to get a couple more notes out of it. In doing this, you'll need to remember that the notes will be displaced by two frets on this string, so it's a good idea to get some practice in before trying it out on a gig!

Drop D tuning
(low to high) D-A-D-G

ABOUT THE AUTHOR

A native of Great Britain, **Scott Barnard** graduated from Trinity College of Music, London, with a performance diploma in classical trumpet. He then went on to be awarded a jazz scholarship on bass guitar.

Over the past 20 years, Scott's playing career has been quite diverse, including engagements such as *Les Misérables*, *Reach Out* (Motown/Temptations national theatre tours), *The Chicago Blues Brothers*, the QE2, function bands, *Opus One* big band, small jazz ensembles, orchestras, and solo recitals.

As a music instructor, Scott has taught many individuals and groups of all ages, in schools and privately, on a variety of instruments. He is the author of *101 Trumpet Tips* (Hal Leonard Corporation; HL00312082).

Scott is also in demand as an arranger, and has provided arrangements for the Raymond Gubbay orchestra, *Don't Forget the Lyrics* (Sky TV), *Sing If You Can* (ITV), and London Orchestrations.

BASS BUILDERS

A series of technique book/audio packages created for the purposeful building and development of your chops. Each volume is written by an expert in that particular technique. And with the inclusion of audio, the added dimension of hearing exactly how to play particular grooves and techniques make these truly like private lessons.

BASS FOR BEGINNERS *INCLUDES TAB*
by Glenn Letsch
00695099 Book/CD Pack........................$19.95

BASS GROOVES *INCLUDES TAB*
by Jon Liebman
00696028 Book/Online Audio $19.99

BASS IMPROVISATION *INCLUDES TAB*
by Ed Friedland
00695164 Book/Online Audio $19.99

BLUES BASS *INCLUDES TAB*
by Jon Liebman
00695235 Book/Online Audio $19.99

BUILDING WALKING BASS LINES
by Ed Friedland
00695008 Book/Online Audio $19.99

**RON CARTER –
BUILDING JAZZ BASS LINES**
00841240 Book/Online Audio $19.99

DICTIONARY OF BASS GROOVES *INCLUDES TAB*
by Sean Malone
00695266 Book/Online Audio $14.95

EXPANDING WALKING BASS LINES
by Ed Friedland
00695026 Book/Online Audio $19.99

FINGERBOARD HARMONY FOR BASS
by Gary Willis
00695043 Book/Online Audio $17.99

FUNK BASS *INCLUDES TAB*
by Jon Liebman
00699348 Book/Online Audio $19.99

FUNK/FUSION BASS *INCLUDES TAB*
by Jon Liebman
00696553 Book/Online Audio $24.99

HIP-HOP BASS *INCLUDES TAB*
by Josquin des Prés
00695589 Book/Online Audio $15.99

JAZZ BASS
by Ed Friedland
00695084 Book/Online Audio $17.99

**JERRY JEMMOTT –
BLUES AND RHYTHM &
BLUES BASS TECHNIQUE** *INCLUDES TAB*
00695176 Book/CD Pack........................$24.99

JUMP 'N' BLUES BASS *INCLUDES TAB*
by Keith Rosier
00695292 Book/Online Audio $17.99

THE LOST ART OF COUNTRY BASS *INCLUDES TAB*
by Keith Rosier
00695107 Book/Online Audio $19.99

PENTATONIC SCALES FOR BASS *INCLUDES TAB*
by Ed Friedland
00696224 Book/Online Audio $19.99

REGGAE BASS *INCLUDES TAB*
by Ed Friedland
00695163 Book/Online Audio $16.99

'70S FUNK & DISCO BASS *INCLUDES TAB*
by Josquin des Prés
00695614 Book/Online Audio $16.99

**SIMPLIFIED SIGHT-READING
FOR BASS** *INCLUDES TAB*
by Josquin des Prés
00695085 Book/Online Audio $17.99

6-STRING BASSICS *INCLUDES TAB*
by David Gross
00695221 Book/Online Audio $14.99

HAL•LEONARD®

halleonard.com

Prices, contents and availability subject to change without notice; All prices are listed in U.S. funds